ONEAWEEK

Behind the Music

Buck Bowen

TABLE OF CONTENTS

PREFACE

"Everything is a Jericho mile for you," The Wolfman, Jack France said.

"What do you mean?" I asked.

"You're always like, 'How can I make this more difficult? I know. I'll ride a unicycle and rap! I know. I'll jump rope and freestyle!'"

In retrospect, that's probably why I'm doing this oneAweek music project. I set a ridiculous goal to be accomplished in an unreasonable amount of time and then go for it.

I wanted to write this book for a few reasons.

First, I base a lot of my motivational content on books and seminars, and I wanted to give those authors and speakers credit. I also wanted to share their inspiring wisdom in hopes that others may benefit.

Secondly, I wanted to shed light on my own darkness.

The third reason, which has shown itself recently, is because – well, despite still releasing one song and video a week, trying to build my video production business, working on magic, and being a good partner – I had to ask myself, "How can I make this *more* difficult?"

INTRODUCTION

This book is about the inspiration and influence behind the oneAweek music project. As of August 2018, I've released one song and video every Monday for 70 weeks in a row.

What follows are brief backstories to eight of my favorite songs and an in-depth annotation of their lyrics. I'll share insight into what gets me out of bed, what keeps me there, and some of the most eye-opening and life-changing advice I've received.

I'll also share the darker and often shameful aspects of my inner struggles.

I've been making music my whole life. I've released five CDs and one vinyl record. When people ask, "What do you do?" I've always answered, "I'm passionate about music."

The problem was that since 2015 I hadn't made much music. This hypocrisy was eating away at me. In April of 2017 that all changed.

I was listening to episode 203 of Gary Vaynerchuk's video blog *DailyVee*.

"It's documenting over creating," he said. "It's just volume. If you're good enough, it will happen.

"You flat out wouldn't have made it 20 years ago. It was just too many gatekeepers. But now the market's the gatekeeper, and the Internet's the middleman.

"Now what's holding people back is that they're using the old model. They think they've got to put out an album every three years, but they need to be putting out a song every day.

"You may not be good enough to put out a song every day. But if you're good enough to put a song out every other day, then *that's* what you do. If you're not good enough to do that, then you put out a song every three days. Whatever it is, you've got to put out those songs."*

On April 17th, a week after watching *DailyVee*, I released my first track and video, *What Others Won't Do*.

Pandora's Box Opened

After a couple of weeks, I was already complaining to a friend that I didn't think I was going to make the week's deadline.

"Don't worry," he assured me. "Just do it the following week. If you miss one deadline, it's no big deal."

He was right but for the wrong reason. It wasn't a big deal, *it was a HUGE deal.* If you let yourself slide, you'll end up slipping. I pushed through and got the song out.

After a month, I felt bitter. I wasn't seeing the results I expected and I wasn't getting the attention I thought I deserved. Disgruntled and scrolling through *YouTube,* I saw a Gary Vee video titled, *Overnight Success,* and my whole mentality was about to shift.

I got two significant takeaways from the video: the necessity of backbreaking hard work and a commitment to lifelong patience.

The video opens with Gary saying, "During that period when I was showing up in all these magazines and T.V. shows I got so many emails from friends in high school. All of them were like, 'Hey Gary, remember me from high school? Oh my god you're so lucky!' I wrote back every single one of them and said, 'Let me clarify one thing. I'm not lucky. I worked. I worked every God damned weekend and holiday since I was 14 years old. So you can keep that luck shit in your pocket.

"Every day of my life I get emails from people telling me that they are quitting. They come to me as a last resort to either convince them not to quit or maybe give them confirmation that they should quit.

'Hey Gary, this is Sally. I've been doing my blog now for nine months, and I'm not getting the results I'd like to see or that I was promised. Should I give up?'"

Gary reflects on how sad he is that he never documented his long days and lonely nights building Wine Library T.V.

"Every single weekend while my friends went to Jersey Shore and hooked up with girls or went fishing or threw around the football and lived the leisure life, I was learning the wine business and honing my craft. I was thirty years old before any of you ever saw me."

Gary hammers home the point that if you've started something you love so much and have the audacity to believe it should be your lifelong career. You need to be working for it the rest of your life – not giving up after four months or two years.

"Nothing in life is free. Nothing happens overnight."

After that, I resolved to do this project indefinitely – complaint free.

*Quotes ending with an asterisk have been edited for readability and language while preserving its message to the best of my ability

PART ONE
BEHIND THE MUSIC

ON PROCESS

Perfectionism Is a Flaw

After the first song dropped, I realized my whole approach to making music had to change. I was now in a battle with depleting time, effort, and energy. I began making my schedule around the music instead of the other way around.

Gone were the days of writing elaborate rhyme schemes. No longer could I take the time searching for the perfect bass line or spend a week to tweak a flawless mix.

At first, I worried my quality would suffer and hurt my potential. However, with a hard deadline and a substantial commitment, I didn't have time to worry. I decided to treat life like a meatball and just roll with it – doing the best I could with what I had while I had it.

Quality Through Quantity

Quality over quantity.

It's a phrase that sounds commendable but only seems to be said by procrastinators who practice neither. I was one of them.

I had a ton of great ideas that I knew would "skyrocket" my success. They just had to be well produced. The problem was that these ideas took forever to create, if at all, and had mediocre results at best – if at all.

A sales training expert and author, Grant Cardone, advocates quality *through* quantity. My outlook changed when I heard him say, "Quantity is more important than quality in the beginning because you aren't going to figure out the quality without the quantity. You won't have the time to worry about the quality if you aren't pushing in quantities high enough to get results."

By applying Grant's counter-intuitive yet straightforward point, I've learned far more about myself and the music making process than if I'd kept waiting for things to be "just right." Not only can I write, record, and produce better with less time and energy but I get more done.

Don't Die with Your Music Still in You

Every week I'm forced to empty another idea from my soul. On several occasions, when pressed for time and having repeated creative failures. I've had to dig up old beats and songs, dust them off, dress them up, and give them a new life.

These were tracks I doubt I would have ever released, and putting them out reminds me of Wayne Dyer's talk about not dying with your music still in you.

"Don't you get to the place at the end of your life where you're lying there like Ivan Ilyich, and you ask the terrifying question, 'What if my whole life has been wrong?'

"There is music in you. It may be in the form of artwork, figuring out how to raise children in daycare centers, or to invent a chip for a computer.

"Whatever you consider to be your music, you've got to let it play. Don't die with your music still in you."*

ON WRITING

It's astonishing what you'll find inside yourself when forced to produce.

When discussing oneAweek, I tell people that after doing so many songs in such a short time, I've realized I mostly write about two topics: GO FOR YOUR GOALS and *fuck it life sucks I'm prob'ly gonna kill myself.* This line always gets a laugh, but it's true.

Before oneAweek, I'd release a couple songs every six months. It was a long, arduous, and emotion-driven process of two steps forward one step back.

I rolled around in a hole of self-doubt and feigned importance. Months later after finally producing a song, I'd emerge from my self-inflicted pit and hail myself as a war hero.

But oneAweek doesn't care about a battle cry, it only cares about victory.

Therefore, I either had to drop the pseudo-struggle or find a way to play out the drama within a week.

Now my writing process usually happens within twenty-four hours or at most spread across a few days. I still strive for writing complex rhymes and witty wordplay, but if I can't write the *best thing* within the first five minutes, I move onto the *next best thing*. If I can't do that, then I just do *the thing*. It's the same process for making the beat.

A quick note on *the thing*. Back when I'd hit the gym a few times a week, I'd have a set routine (best thing). However, some nights I'd feel drained and only do a partial workout (next best thing). Other nights I'd refuse to leave the house, so I'd force myself to go to the gym just to touch the wall (the thing).

Touching the wall isn't exactly a workout, but I wasn't wholly letting myself off the hook. On a few occasions, I just decided to exercise since I was already there.

ON PRODUCING

My primary means of making music has always been sampling. For example, I'd take drums from a funk record, bass from jazz, and piano from classical. I'd change the pitch, add effects, and reverse or layer the samples to make unique sounds.

These techniques have worked well for me over the years, but they're time-consuming, and like most creative endeavors they offer no guarantees.

I found myself looking for ways to produce more efficiently (sorry "real" artists). I began to focus more on using software synthesizers and virtual instruments despite having next to no musical training.

The key for me, pun intended, was a reliance on just three notes that I could vary in tone, length, and pattern.

Because of this, many of my songs sound very similar, and I've been called the Danny Elfman of Hip Hop.

However, I'm in good company. A comedy website, College Humor, produced a video called *Tim Burton's Secret Formula* that pokes fun at Elfman's notably familiar sound.

C, C#, and F. Those are the three notes. On the computer's keyboard they're the A, W, and F keys.

In my music production software, the middle row of keys beginning with A and ending with L represent the white keys of a piano. The W E, T Y U, and I O P are the black keys.

As much as I'm attracted to the sonic quality of the notes, I speculate that I chose them due to the natural resting position of the left hand on the computer's keyboard.

I take pride in doing so much with so little.

I can relate to Johnny Cash's bass player Marshall Grant who was once asked how they came up with their signature "boom-chicka-boom" sound.

He replied, "It's all we knew how to play."

ON VIDEO

It wasn't my intention to make a video with every song, I just wanted something to supplement the music because I thought it'd get more attention.

I think it helps, but it adds between four to twelve more hours of work per week.

I welcome the challenge though because it's improved my organizing, editing, and storyboarding skills.

Sometimes it even influences the music. If I have two subjects I want to write about, but one of them is harder to conceptualize visually, I'll go with the easier one.

I have a set of video styles I use based on a few factors:

Music Video: this is the best but most difficult as it often requires lots of resources like time, money, and people.

Stock Footage: challenging because it requires lots of searching for quality clips that can be logically put together. Some of the earlier videos feature a combination of stock and personal footage.

Movie Montage: this requires lots of searching, but sometimes I get lucky, and it just hits. The video for *Overboard* is a perfect example.

Video Montage: same as above but instead of movies it could be a commercial, viral video, documentary, or something random I find online.

Looped Footage: usually this happens when I've found video that works, but there's not enough to last the length of the song. I try to find five distinct but related clips that I can loop for the intro, chorus, verse, and outro.

Lyric Video: I only choose this option if one of the others is proving too difficult. Typing out all the lyrics, adjusting fonts, and adding motion to the words can quickly get laborious.

PART TWO
BEHIND THE LYRICS

WHAT OTHERS WON'T DO

You must be willing to do the things today others won't do
In order to have the things tomorrow others won't have
You must be willing to do the things today others won't do
In order to have the things tomorrow others won't have

It's not supposed to be easy, why should it be?
Put in the requisite hours, plus another two or three
Nobody cares if you've got time or not
Your passion needs to eat so feed it to make the crying stop

Check your reflection make sure the mirror works
The Universe really owes you nothing, 'cause it was here first
You better get it together never settle for lesser
It's either now, or it's never

This isn't forever; your life is finite
So get your mind right before the time's right
Go 'head take a chance, shake your plans
You never know, by letting go you may advance

'Cause here's the ugly truth
Most of us are trading five days just for two
Feeling stuck like glue, so what to do?
Anything, do it now, something new, just get up and move

You must be willing to do the things today others won't do
In order to have the things tomorrow others won't have
You must be willing to do the things today others won't do
In order to have the things tomorrow others won't have

You're on a mission with wide eyes and big vision
Practice your craft at least ten minutes
I promise you can find the time
Just do it right before you close your eyes at night

Do you want it or not? If you don't, then forget it
If you do, then let's get it, you've got to be committed
Sure it's a challenge trying to hit the nail
But who needs balance? When you're trying to tip the scale

So what if you don't hit your target
The worst likely to happen is that you end up where you started
So try, try, try again, keep firing
Attacking life like a pirate ship

Go get them, full momentum
No excuses, no regrets, and no bullshitting
You say you'll do it, but it never happens
Just remember, your future is full of your present actions

You must be willing to do the things today others won't do
In order to have the things tomorrow others won't have
You must be willing to do the things today others won't do
In order to have the things tomorrow others won't have

WHAT OTHERS WON'T DO

"Some people dream of success while others wake up and work hard at it." – Winston Churchill

This song was sparked by a conversation with a friend about pursuing challenging goals. To help us see through our excuses, I played some clips from Les Brown's 1998 *Armed and Dangerous* motivational speech. It's from this seminar that I heard the quote that became the basis for this track.

> "You must be willing to do the things today others won't do
> In order to have the things tomorrow others won't have"

This is a direct sample of Les Brown's voice. I wonder if his quote was inspired by Albert E. N. Gray's pamphlet, *The Common Denominator of Success*.

In the abridged audiobook of *No Excuses*, Brian Tracy summarizes Albert's findings: "The common denominator of success is quite simple. Successful people make a habit of doing what unsuccessful people don't like to do. What is it that unsuccessful people don't like to do? Well, it turned out to be the same thing that successful people don't like to do either, but they do it anyway because they recognize that that's the price of success."

> It's not supposed to be easy, why should it be?

We waste time and invite pain by wishing that reality was something other than what it is.

Wayne Dyer in his book *Pulling Your Own Strings* wrote a

whole chapter on how we routinely confuse our judgments for reality and how it negatively affects us. Much of our suffering is self-inflicted. By distinguishing between reality and our judgment of it, we can avoid a lot of needless pain.

> The Universe really owes you nothing,
> 'Cause it was here first

"Don't believe the world owes you a living. The world owes you nothing; it was here first." – Robert J. Burdette

> This isn't forever; your life is finite
> So get your mind right before the time's right

"Leap and grow your wings on the way down." – Les Brown

> 'Cause here's the ugly truth
> Most of us are trading five days just for two

The Weekend Warrior mentality is detrimental to happiness in that it suppresses five days of positive emotions for two that may never come. See my rant on how to feel Friday on Tuesday at the end of this book.

Although I don't subscribe to any religion, I admire the Old Testament God's work ethic: 6 days labor, 1-day rest.

Grant Cardone said, "That one-day off is for those who've actually worked."

> Feeling stuck like glue, so what to do?
> Anything, do it now, something new, just get up and move

How many times have you said that you would do X task if you were only motivated? Unfortunately, it doesn't work that way.

Zig Ziglar pointed out: "Motivation *follows* the action." First, you act, and then you get motivated.

Tony Robbins demonstrates this with an exercise. First, you sit slumped in a chair for a few minutes frowning with your head resting between your hands.

How do you feel? Probably sluggish and sad.

Then, stand up and do a series of jumping jacks while yelling.

Now how do you feel? Perhaps a bit a silly but for sure not lethargic.

To quote Robbins, "How you move is how you feel."

You're on a mission with wide eyes and big vision
Practice your craft at least ten minutes
I promise you can find the time
Just do it right before you close your eyes at night

You're lying if you say you don't have ten minutes. Whether your passion is sports, art, or competitive dog grooming, it's not a question of whether you have ten minutes but whether or not you are willing to sacrifice for your goals.

Dribble the ball on your way to school.

Use your commute time to create a song in your head.

Listen to a lecture while you're waiting in a line.

Skip lunch to practice test questions or study flashcards.

Read on the toilet instead of checking social media.

Get up early. Stay up late.

What if you knew you had to practice your passion ten minutes a day or your mother's head would be cut off?

You'd get it done.

Do you want it or not? If you don't, then forget it
If you do, then let's get it, you've got to be committed

Tony Robbins points out that change happens instantly. It's our *deciding* to change that usually takes a while.

My goal with the above lyric is to encourage you to stop torturing yourself with indecision. If you've got a goal and you're committed, quit bitching about falling off the horse. Either walk away or dust yourself off and giddy up.

But who needs balance? When you're trying to tip the scale

"If you become comfortable, you take less action. When you take less action, you stop pushing to fulfill your potential. The person who limits their potential success will limit what they will do to create and keep it." – Grant Cardone

So what if you don't hit your target
The worst likely to happen
Is that you end up where you started

"Failure often just means ending up where you started." – Unknown

You say you'll do it, but it never happens
Just remember, your future is full of your present actions

"Your future is full of your present actions." – Chinese proverb

Earl Shoaff and Dennis Gabor say something equally compelling, "If you want to know what you'll reap, look at what you're sowing," and "The best way to predict the future is to create it."

WORK THE DREAM

9 to 5 work the job
5 to 9 work the dream
'Cause luxury comes at the cost
Of killing your hopes and your dreams

So what have you done today?
Having some fun today what about work?
Oh after you eat a meal?
Come on man keep it real do the work first

You talk about passion, but I don't see action
Man, all I hear's words
The heck with excuses let's get up and do this
And put in the work

Nobody's going to come and give you opportunities
You got to take initiative and make the possibilities
To put yourself in a position where you prob'ly will succeed
I'm telling you the facts it doesn't happen accidentally

Kick in the discipline got to commit to it
Take a deep breath
'Cause everybody living has an option that was given
Suffer pain of discipline or the pain of regret

9 to 5 work the job
5 to 9 work the dream
'Cause luxury comes at the cost
Of killing your hopes and your dreams

So who do you want to be?
Someone who gets what they want?
Or one of the losers?
Who makes excuses a lot

And where do you want to be?
On top with the winners?
Or down at the bottom?
In the dumps having lunch with the quitters?

Stop pissing your weekend away
Then complaining how you hate your job
When you won't even give yourself ten minutes
Practicing that which you love

Force your physiology
You got to go beyond your body's limits to accomplish things
You cannot let your mental challenges stop your dream
Everything is hard before it's easy just start it, please!

9 to 5 work the job
5 to 9 work the dream
'Cause luxury comes at the cost
Of killing your hopes and your dreams

WORK THE DREAM

"Make mistakes of ambition, not sloth."
– Machiavelli

"Work the Dream" is one of my three favorites from the oneAweek project. It's a bass heavy trap beat with a chopper style flow.

All the elements came together despite the beat style and rhyme scheme not being my strong suit. It was an exercise in producing, writing, and especially delivery.

Rapping fast is easy. It only becomes difficult when you make a concerted effort to enunciate and stay on beat.

"I don't want to hear about this two job thing, right? '9 to 5, I don't have time.' If you want this, work 9 to 5, spend a couple of hours with the family. You kiss the dog, and you go to town. That's it. It's not going to happen any other way. If you want this, work! That's how you get it."

This snippet comes from Gary Vaynerchuk's keynote speech at the Web 2.0 Expo in New York, 2008.

9 to 5 work the job
5 to 9 work the dream

My mom, inspired by her Amway meetings, always said this to me growing up. Thanks, mom!

'Cause luxury comes at the cost
Of killing your hopes and your dreams

I heard Tai Lopez say this in an online discussion of Seneca's book, *On the Shortness of Life*.

So what have you done today?
Having some fun today what about work?
Oh after you eat a meal
C'mon man keep it real do the work first

Dinner Before Dessert is a concept by Brian Tracy in which he makes a powerful analogy between the logical order of meals and self-discipline.

You talk about passion, but I don't see action
Man, all I hear's words

This is a jab at myself. Before the oneAweek project, the number of times I claimed to be passionate about music vastly outweighed the number of times I made music.

Nobody's going to come and give you opportunities
You got to take initiative and make the possibilities

Inspired by a seminar from Owen Cook, a.k.a. RSD Tyler, where he said, "No one's going to put you on. You have to put yourself on. Success is about quiet little actions. It's not this big ra-ra speech where you do this *one* thing, then something big happens."*

It's embarrassing to think of how much time I've pissed away griping about how if I only had someone to help me or if I had a record label recognize my talents, *then* I'd be successful.

Complaining is more comfortable than committing, which is why most people do one and not the other.

You must create your own luck.

Suffer pain of discipline or the pain of regret

"We must all suffer one of two pains: the pain of discipline or the pain of regret. The difference is discipline weighs ounces while regret weighs tons." – Jim Rohn

So who do you want to be?
Someone who gets what they want?
Or one of the losers?
Who makes excuses a lot

For an exhaustive list of excuses, please read Napoleon Hill's, *"Fifty-Seven" Famous Alibis by Old Man If.*

Stop pissing your weekend away
Then complaining how you hate your job

How many of us act like zombies during the week?

We groan about all the things we'd do if we didn't have to work, then the weekend comes, and we rush to ~~celebrate~~ medicate ourselves with Gutterade, puke fuel, and disco biscuits.

How many of us choose instead to work the dream? The choice is yours, and it's a powerful one.

Force your physiology
You got to go beyond your body's limits to accomplish things

"I'm tired, and I don't want to do it. I've got a million reasons not to do it, but if I can't make myself go do this, how am I going to live my dreams? I've found that if I miss one day; I'll miss every day." – RSD Tyler from his video, *What Is Success?*

Everything is hard before it's easy just start it, please!

"Everything is hard before it's easy." – Goethe

"If you do what is easy your life will be hard. If you do what is hard your life will be easy." – Les Brown

THEY SAY

They say, "I ain't seen you at the club"
I say, "I ain't seen you at the bank"
They say, "You only live once"
I say, "It's not living if it's fake"

We spend money we don't have, on things we don't need
To impress people we don't even like, and that's weak
Pretty car, ugly payment
We've got to go into debt to make a statement

And you know what they say, "You can't take this…
Money with you when you die, so why save it?"
Um, of course you can, doofus
All we need to know is how big the Egyptian tomb is

Stop pretending
When you say, "live a little,"
What you mean is, "lots of spending"
Dawg, you got to stop it
The point of a budget is to patch a hole in the pocket

You sleep like you're rich
I'm up like I'm broke and I'm going for it
Here's some cry-nancial advice for you babies
Take your excuses and put them in savings

They say, "I ain't seen you at the club"
I say, "I ain't seen you at the bank"
They say, "You only live once"
I say, "It's not living if it's fake"

You gave a half day's work for a full day's pay
New shoes on your feet, but your rent's always late
Claiming you live check-to-check, saying, "I'm broke"
Yet it seems you have money to buy things like nice clothes

Some people live to regret
Dive into a pool of credit, drown, swimming in debt
Found injured and wet, and I don't mean to diss you
If you're getting raises every year, then money's not the issue

It's how you manage it
The amount really isn't as important as how you handle it
I'm talking honestly
Look at broke athletes and winners who lost the lottery

Grind while they rest
Study when they party trying to impress
Keep showing up, and you're bound to succeed
And one day they'll see you live like they dream

They say, "I ain't seen you at the club"
I say, "I ain't seen you at the bank"
They say, "You only live once"
I say, "It's not living if it's fake"

THEY SAY

The glorification of material things is very common in Rap & Hip-Hop music. "They Say" calls out the emptiness of this superficial mentality.

I fashioned the track around Lil Dicky's song, "$ave Dat Money." While lyrically he takes a comedic angle, I chose a finger-wagging priggish approach.

"A guy told me recently, 'Grant man, I don't see you at the club anymore.' I said, 'Bro, I don't see you at the bank at all.'"

I directly sampled Grant Cardone's voice from his video, *Get Your Money Right Grant Rant*.

They say, "You only live once"

People who use statements like this are usually trying to justify or make themselves feel less guilty about making stupid choices.

We spend money we don't have, on things we don't need
To impress people we don't even like

"We buy things we don't need with money we don't have to impress people we don't like." – Dave Ramsey, *The Total Money Makeover: A Proven Plan for Financial Fitness.*

> And you know what they say, "You can't take this…
> Money with you when you die, so why save it?"

Only broke people say this to shame you into giving them your ~~labor~~ money.

> Um, of course you can, doofus

Please take a moment to appreciate that your favorite rapper just used the classic, highly juvenile schoolyard diss: Doofus.

> All we need to know is how big the Egyptian tomb is

The Egyptians took gold, silver, chariots, boats, jewelry, and a host of other things to the grave.

Do not be pressured into giving up your money by a friend or relative who says you can't take it with you when you die. Tell them they can have it when you're dead, but they'll have to dig it up.

They won't go near a shovel because that would require work. Instead, they'll bitch about how stingy you were.

> When you say, "live a little,"
> What you mean is, "lots of spending"

Some of us are cheap or frugal to the point of missing out on inexpensive, positive experiences.

However, the people who say, "It's only a dollar," are the people who don't have one. *Only a dollar* a hundred times is a hundred dollars.

Jim Rohn gives a talk called, "What a Child Should Do with a Dollar." It'll completely change the way you think about money, and I suggest you find it online.

The point of a budget is to patch a hole in the pocket

Nobody likes to budget because it feels restrictive, but that's the point. Your problem isn't saving money, it's misspending it.

You sleep like you're rich, I'm up like I'm broke

"You sleep like you're rich, I'm up like I'm broke." – Grant Cardone.

Here's some cry-nancial advice for you babies
Take your excuses and put them in savings

This Buck Bowen original wordplay is aimed at those who whine about their financial situation and do nothing about it except invest in excuses.

You gave a half day's work for a full day's pay

"Wherever you are, put it on. Don't give somebody half a job for a day's pay." – Jim Rohn

New shoes on your feet, but your rent's always late

"Every choice you make is a statement about your true values and priorities." – Brian Tracy

Claiming you live check-to-check, saying, "I'm broke"
Yet it seems you have money to buy things like nice clothes

Economist Walter E. Williams, writing in support of the free market, notes how in poor neighborhoods you see nice clothing, good food, and expensive cars, but no decent schools.
    The reason is that clothing, food, and cars are

distributed by the market mechanism, while schools are distributed by the political mechanism.

Dive into a pool of credit, drown, swimming in debt

In *The Total Money Makeover* Dave Ramsey lays out a simple and effective plan for eliminating debt. No matter how many cards you have, you must put ALL your money towards the credit card with the highest interest rate while paying the minimum on the others. Repeat until all debt is erased and don't make the mistake of continuing to use credit.

Invest your "extra" money. You have no excuse because you've already been living without it.

If you're getting raises every year, then money's not the issue

I have friends who receive a raise every year but are just as broke as the day I met them.

A derivative of Parkinson's Law states, "Expenses rise in direct proportion to income."

We tend to spend a little more than we make, so it's easy to see how people remain perpetually poor.

Break Parkinson's Law.

It's how you manage it
The amount really isn't as important as how you handle it

"It's not your salary that makes you rich; it's your spending habits." – Charles A. Jaffe

Grind while they rest
Study when they party trying to impress
Keep showing up, and you're bound to succeed
And one day they'll see you live like they dream

"Grind while they rest. Study when they party. You'll live like they dream." – Grant Cardone.

GET STARTED

You want to be on top
The bottom's way too crowded
Stand firm in your vision and goals
'Cause most will try to make you doubt it

We call them crabs in a bucket
People who love to hold you back
And see you stagger and struggling

So what if I'm fumbling? As long as I keep stacking forward
There's going to be some back and forth
I just have to attack with force

I'll take the cuts, scrapes, even the scars
You don't get in life what you want, man
You get what you are

So were you born to win or born to lose?
I know you're feeling worn and bruised
But you must muster up and ignore the boos

So don't think you'll fail
You don't have to travel the beaten path
You can forge your own and leave a trail

No test, no testimony
If you don't give it a shot, you run the risk of never knowing
The coward dies a thousand deaths
So when your final hour's left, will you be drowning in regret?

You don't have to be great to get started
But you have to get started to be great
You don't have to be great to get started
So get started before it's too late

When your dream is big enough, the odds don't matter
Feel the fear and do it anyway, in fact, go faster
Look, if you're headed down the wrong path
You want to find out as quick as possible, so you can stop that

You thought quitting wasn't an option?
Actually, it's not the losers, but winners who quit more often
We don't fail because we aim too high and miss
The reason that we fail's because we often aim too low and hit

You've got to take a risk to win
The most important habit to develop's prob'ly discipline
Grab the stick and shift to drive
If it's worth it, it's worth doing badly till you get it right

Get obsessed, create your goal and reach beyond it
Go the extra mile; you'll notice there're less people on it
Are you committed? 'Cause I ain't going to stop
Even if it means I have to fail my way to the top

You don't have to be great to get started
But you have to get started to be great
You don't have to be great to get started
So get started before it's too late

GET STARTED

"The way to get started is to quit talking and begin doing."
– Walt Disney

It was Sunday evening, and since I still couldn't get a beat to click with the lyrics I nearly missed the deadline for this song.

I was feeling hopeless, so I did what any wise man does in this situation: devolve into absurdity.

I started making a track at 45bpm. This tempo was way too slow, but it sounded unique with Les Brown's voice pitched down.

Reverting back to normality, I doubled the beat's speed to 90bpm, and everything fell into place.

However, the nightmare wasn't over because I still needed to record vocals and create the accompanying music video. I couldn't find a filmmaker at midnight, and this was before I learned how to make lyric videos. Since missing a day wasn't an option, I grabbed a tripod and my iPhone.

The video was a challenge.

First, I didn't have the lyrics memorized.

Second, I was trying to film in the middle of the street in downtown Long Beach.

Third, it was nearing the zombie hour, and this sketchy guy kept riding around on his bike watching me. Out the corner of my eye, I saw him reach down to steal my bag. I turned towards him and he said, "Oh, is this yours?"

"You don't have to be great to get started
But you have to get started to be great"

I directly sampled Les Brown's voice from his *Seminar of the Century* talk.

You want to be on top, the bottom's way too crowded

"Always strive to get on top in life because it's the bottom that's overcrowded." – Les Brown

Stand firm in your vision and goals
'Cause most will try to make you doubt it

Sadly, it's often those closest to us who make us doubt ourselves.

There's a story about Oprah that claims whenever she loses weight she loses friends.

Our efforts to make a positive change can cause friends and family to object because it either makes them feel like they're losing you to a stranger (the new you) or causes them to reflect on how they could be improving but aren't.

I've been guilty of this behavior, but at the time I wasn't even aware of what I was doing.

We call them crabs in a bucket
People who love to hold you back
And see you stagger and struggling

Crab mentality: the analogy in human behavior that members of a group will attempt to reduce the self-confidence and halt the progress of any member who achieves success beyond the others. (Source *Wikipedia*)

So what if I'm fumbling?
As long as I keep stacking forward
There's going to be some back and forth
I just have to attack with force

"When life knocks you down try to land on your back, because if you can look up, you can get up." – Les Brown

You don't get in life what you want, man; you get what you are

"You don't attract what you want. You attract what you are." – Wayne Dyer

So don't think you'll fail
You don't have to travel the beaten path
You can forge your own and leave a trail

"Do not go where the path may lead, go instead where there is no path and leave a trail." – Ralph Waldo Emerson

If you don't give it a shot, you run the risk of never knowing

"You miss 100% of the shots you don't take." – Wayne Gretzky

The coward dies a thousand deaths

"A coward dies a thousand times before his death, but the valiant taste of death but once." – William Shakespeare, *Julius Caesar*

When your dream is big enough, the odds don't matter

"When your dreams are big enough, the odds just don't matter." – JohnA Passaro

When I was 14 years old, I met legendary skateboarder Jeremy Wray. I asked him what he did when he was scared to do a trick.

"I go faster," he answered.

My dad supported this notion by adding, "It's like riding a bike with no hands. It's moving slowly that causes you to crash.

"Winners quit all the time. They just quit the right stuff at the right time." – Seth Godin, *The Dip: A Little Book That Teaches You When to Quit*

"Most people fail in life, not because they aim too high and miss, but because they aim too low and hit." – Les Brown.

Grant Cardone makes an insightful point in his book *The 10X Rule* when he writes, "If you have a $100,000 goal and a million dollar goal, which one do you want to come up short on?"

We often limit our actions based on problems we *think* we have. I volunteered for a charity over Thanksgiving, and one of the other volunteers was having a difficult time. She couldn't seem to scoop a sufficient amount of mashed potatoes.

"Take your scoop and try to get the biggest chunk of mashed potatoes ever," I advised.

"Oh no, I can't do that," she replied. "I don't want to scoop too much."

I pointed out that her problem wasn't scooping "too much," it was scooping "too little." I noted that she *could always scale it back.*

She felt uncomfortable but started giving large scoops. A few plates later, after she really pushed her limits, she was able to give a regular scoop.

Take it to the extreme. *You can always scale it back.*

If it's worth it, it's worth doing badly till you get it right

"Anything worth doing is worth doing poorly – until you can learn to do it well." – Zig Ziglar

Go the extra mile; you'll notice there're less people on it

In Grant Cardone's audiobook *Secrets of Selling*, he discusses the importance of getting out in front of others with a hilarious personal story of being pulled over.

"You were speeding," the officer said.

"Sir, I knew that three miles before you pulled me over. Did you get me when I was topping out at 140mph?" Grant replied.

"No, I got you at 112mph. Why were you going so fast?"

"I was driving around with these other people, and they're crazy. I had to get out in front of them!"

Grant then speaks to his audience, "I don't want to ride with them because that's the middle. I'd rather get a ticket. You want to get out in front or get a driver, one of the two."

Are you committed? 'Cause I ain't going to stop
Even if it means I have to fail my way to the top

"I'd prob'ly quit, if I only knew how to give up." – Buck Bowen, *Aluminumb*

KEEP MOVING

What am I supposed to say?
Sometimes I feel like giving up; I'm going to throw it all away
I'm running out of jokes to make
I've tried to move, but always end up living in a hopeless state

I smile, trying not to show the pain
Paranoid that my friends are annoyed, they prob'ly know it's fake
Feeling numb like Novocain
Introverted, out my mind, trying not to go insane

I think too much, and my action's almost non-existent
No, I act too often without thinking of the consequences
Feeling nauseous, livid, this toxic venom is stress
But I guess that's just the cost of living

They don't get it; it's not something a quote can fix
Motivation's overrated, I don't think I can cope with it
I try, but I fumble
Dark days and lonely nights with no light in the tunnel

I got to keep moving, even though I keep losing
Even though I keep losing, I got to keep moving
I got to keep moving, even though I keep losing
Even though I keep losing, I got to keep moving

I don't mean to be sounding feeble
But sometimes I feel the most alone amongst a crowd of people
Overanalyzing everything
It's such a vicious cycle getting stuck inside a memory

And I can't seem to let it go
Thinking *if I could do it over* things would be better you know?
I wouldn't be in the pain I'm in
But knowing me, I'd blow it see and prob'ly do the same again

Is this the myth of Sisyphus? 'Cause if it is
I'm not sure I'll be able to persist with it
Every morning, a weight on my chest, awake and in bed
Covered by the pain of regret

It's hard to move into the future
When you're anchored to the past and always feeling like a loser
I guess I just got to keep showing up
'Cause it's the only way I've got a chance for things to open up

I got to keep moving, even though I keep losing
Even though I keep losing, I got to keep moving
I got to keep moving, even though I keep losing
Even though I keep losing, I got to keep moving

KEEP MOVING

"Depression isn't about,
'Woe is me, my life is this, that and the other,' it's like
having the worst flu all day that you just can't kick."
– Robbie Williams

I never intended to write and release a song so personal. It's my most vulnerable track to date, and I was reluctant to put it out for fear of judgment, sounding cliché, and worrying people.

But unexpected things happen when an unwavering commitment meets an unbreakable deadline – or when you run out of ra-ra motivational content.

I love the way the lo-fi drums, sorrowful strings, and downcast lyrics ebb and flow.

The visuals perfectly capture the song's raw emotion and vulnerability.

I really like how professional the video looks despite having no budget. My only equipment was a tripod, an iPhone, and my bed. All the camera movements were done, frame-by-frame, in my editing program.

None of my concerns about the song's reception happened. Many people told me how they could relate to the lyrics and others said it was my best work.

What am I supposed to say?
Sometimes I feel like giving up; I'm going to throw it all away

The most commonly used sentence in my journals is probably, "I don't know." Sometimes *throwing it all away* is just a cathartic expression. Other times, it means what it says.

I've tried to move, but always end up living in a hopeless state

This is a reference to a lyric from the song "All Things" on my album *Phone Sex II/Second Glance*.

"You want to run away from the place you're living in, but you'll find your problems follow you because they lay within. It ain't easy; it'll take some time. Instead of relocating, try changing your state of mind."

> I smile, trying not to show the pain
> Paranoid that my friends are annoyed
> They prob'ly know it's fake

I've gotten better over the years, but there have been times when I became immobilized by irrational thoughts of what people thought of me. 98% of the time it was solely in my head, and the other 2% didn't matter.

It's like that old saying, "My life has been full of terrible misfortunes, most of which never happened."

> I think too much, and my action's almost non-existent
> No, I act too often without thinking of the consequences

"Most problems in life are because of two reasons: we act without thinking, or we keep thinking without acting." – Unknown

> They don't get it; it's not something a quote can fix
> Motivation's overrated, I don't think I can cope with it

Sometimes I feel like a hypocrite. On the one hand, I'm yelling, "Get inspired and go for your goals!" On the other hand, I'm depressed with suicidal thoughts.

I believe the motivational content helps to offset my negative thinking and feelings of despair when getting through the day feels like a struggle to survive.

I don't mean to be sounding feeble
But sometimes I feel the most alone amongst a crowd of people

I typically don't go to bars or clubs. However, when I do, it's not uncommon for my over-analytical mind to read into everything and twist itself into knots with thoughts such as:

What's the point of all of this?

Why are these people here spending the little money they have on piss flavored water engaged in seemingly meaningless conversation?

Why are they acting in ways they wouldn't if the lights were on?

Why do they move like that to that music?

Why do they move at all?

What's so funny about what she said?

It'd be one thing if these questions came from a basis of curiosity, but they don't.

When I see beautiful women and good-looking men at a club, a dark cloud of judgment, fear, and insecurity lingers over me. The confusion becomes envy and resentment, which turns into extreme doubt and self-hatred. It's a vicious cycle. It's not pretty. It's not admirable.

However, it has gotten better over the years.

Overanalyzing everything
It's such a vicious cycle getting stuck inside a memory

There is a line from my first album, *Phone Sex I/First Perception*, which says, "The past is your enemy attacking your memory."

I released this album at a time in my life when I was feeling like a guilt-ridden piece of shit. It had become a top priority to degrade myself.

Despite my disdain for life suicide was out of the question, but only because it would have ended the very thing I subsisted on – self-flagellation.

42

I lost a few years of my life with the amount of self-loathing and negativity in which I had engaged.

I deeply resonated with R.A. the Rugged Man's song, "Smith Haven Mall," and I listened to it daily on repeat.

I've worked my way out of this pit, but there's still progress to be made.

And I can't seem to let it go
Thinking if I could do it over things would be better you know?
I wouldn't be in the pain I'm in
But knowing me, I'd blow it see, and prob'ly do the same again

Insanity: doing the same thing repeatedly and expecting a different result.

I believe the reason that we tell ourselves we'd "do it the right way" if we could "do it over," is merely to absolve our present feelings of regret.

If you're not doing things the right way now, it's doubtful you would do them correctly if given another chance.

If you're in your 40's and going to college for the first time, while wishing you'd studied more in high school, but you're still not studying, it's likely you'd do the same if you could go back.

All you can do is study more today.

But is the solution always that simple? What if you were a terrible person towards a close friend many years ago, and that person has since died? You can't go back to the past, and you can't start treating them better in the present. So what *can* you do? I'll come back to that.

Although most of my regrets are about personal choices I *didn't* make, the latter example is the type of scenario I beat myself up over.

It's this type of situation that my self-loathing brain acts like there's no easy answer for. Therefore, I remain stuck in a self-made web of harsh criticism with no hope of escape.

I believe the answer is in knowing what's within your control and what isn't, and then concerning yourself with only the former.

You can't change your past behavior towards others. But you can be a decent person now to everyone you know and meet.

> Is this the myth of Sisyphus? 'Cause if it is
> I'm not sure I'll be able to persist with it

Food for thought: J. Nigro Sansonese speculates that the origin of the name "Sisyphus" is onomatopoetic of the continual back-and-forth whispering sound ("siss phuss") made by the breath in the nasal passages. The repetitive inhalation-exhalation cycle is described esoterically in the myth as an up-down motion of Sisyphus and his boulder on a hill. (Source *Wikipedia*)

> I guess I just got to keep showing up
> 'Cause it's the only way I've got a chance for things to open up

Many years ago, my friend and fellow writer Stephen R. Whelan said something very profound about suicide.

"What being alive will always offer that death cannot, is chance. A chance to push through whatever darkness is affecting you. It not only offers an opportunity to remember what being happy means, but also something even more powerful – the chance to make meaning out of suffering."*

TEMPEST

Every third thought be my grave
Relinquish the magic, imagine a day
Devoid of the noise from the gnats and the flies
No more aching over moments that keep passing me by

Floating in a primitive impetus
Annoyingly the buoyancy's a curse, not a benefit
How can I contend with it
Drowning in my thoughts on a plot to get rid of it

Feeling crushed by the abyss down deep
But on the surface, it's like an itch just out of reach
Even though I've enacted some of the best advice
My mind's still overstimulated; body feels anesthetized

I just want to rest my eyes
Wondering if nothing's right, then what else is there left in life?
Find the void and fill it with a grin
Can't escape the thought it's all just Robin Williams in the end

I lie in bed stressed, tired and awake
I'm not sure how much more of this I can take
I lie in bed stressed, tired and awake
I'm not sure how much more of this I can take

I can feel it in my chest, deep within my bones
This numbness is a plague, and it's spreading to my soul
The light is getting dim, even though the sun is shining
I guess darkness has a way of sending shadows to come find me

Make it stop; I don't want nothing more
I'm under the weather trying to get over a thunderstorm
I used to think it was the norm
My mother gave me life, but I'm really not sure what it's for

Irrelevant, loser
Convincing myself, it'll get better in the future
It's prob'ly a lie
But I say it anyway, 'cause it helps me get by

I tried so hard and got so far
Stretched myself thin, then pulled apart
I tried so hard for the goals I was after
But in the end, it doesn't even matter

I lie in bed stressed, tired and awake
I'm not sure how much more of this I can take
I lie in bed stressed, tired and awake
I'm not sure how much more of this I can take

TEMPEST

"There is peace, even in the storm."
– Vincent van Gogh

I watched a South East Asian rendition of *The Tempest* (the first Shakespearean play I'd ever seen) and spent most of it stuck in my head pondering my mortality, questioning the meaning of life, and growing ever consumed with aging and regret as the play unfolded.

This song is the product of that night's head-trip.

For the beat, I wanted a gritty bass line that didn't hit where you'd expect. I especially love the snare with its beefy reverberated clap. Both "Likwit Fusion" and "Whenimondamic" by Lootpack were influences despite the final track having little resemblance.

Every third thought be my grave

"And thence retire me to my Milan, where every third thought shall be my grave." – Prospero, *The Tempest*

Relinquish the magic, imagine a day
Devoid of the noise from the gnats and the flies
No more aching over moments that keep passing me by

I long for a day when I can breathe, and the inappropriate thoughts, overanalyzing, and unhealthy focus on the past no longer torment me.

Floating in a primitive impetus
Annoyingly the buoyancy's a curse, not a benefit

At times, especially when the monkey mind has saddled up the lizard brain, to be alive feels more like a punishment than a privilege.

How can I contend with it
Drowning in my thoughts on a plot to get rid of it

French philosopher René Descartes said, "I think. Therefore I am." However, he forgot one word, "I think. Therefore I am *suffering*."

Even though I've enacted some of the best advice
My mind's still overstimulated; body feels anesthetized

My intense focus on motivational material helps curb my incessant negative thinking. It's a way to keep the demons caged, but sometimes the self-help stuff, despite its truth and power, feels insufficient to prevent the gates from opening.

Irrelevant, loser, convincing myself, it'll get better in the future
It's prob'ly a lie, but I say it anyway, 'cause it helps me get by

"Truth Before Comfort" was my motto for many years. I'm not sure how firmly I believe that anymore.

> I tried so hard and got so far
> Stretched myself thin, then pulled apart
> I tried so hard for the goals I was after
> But in the end, it doesn't even matter

Written around the time of Chester Bennington's death, these last lines are a homage to the Linkin Park song, "In the End."

MEPHISTO

What should I be pissed about today?
It's best you don't come around my way
I'm not feeling in a talking mood
I'm feeling awful, awful, all consumed

By the media, by all the thoughts I'm thinking of
Overstimulated, can't concentrate, and I'm feeling numb
When will it end?
Losing hope, reminiscing of Robin Williams again

This is typical
I've been around enough to know this stuff is often cyclical
But that doesn't give me hope
That just means I need to paddle long enough to keep afloat

I'd trade a year for a moment to breathe
But I suppose I do that anyway, poor pitiful me
Feeling shitty and dull
Not sure how much light is left in this flickering bulb

Hello darkness, my old friend
I came to talk to, talk to you again
If misery loves company
You must be, must be the one for me

I don't expect things to be perfect
In fact, I often expect that my chest is full of stress and hurting
I'm not sure the pressure's worth it
Hectic, nervous, fumbling through life to find a better purpose

(I try) But my head is bursting
Chronically controlled by demonically possessive urges
It's for the better I don't shed the surface
You don't really want to know what sits below this heavy burden

I'm catastrophizing again
Maddening I admit, passively I resist
I should just do what I ought to
But this circular logic got me stuck in a thought-loop

Misery in the present, regret about the past
The future isn't any better don't know whether I can last
I don't mean to be so candid when
I talk about my resignation letter to be handed in

Hello darkness, my old friend
I came to talk to, talk to you again
If misery loves company
You must be, must be the one for me

MEPHISTO

"It is always consoling to think of suicide:
In that way, one gets through many a bad night."
– Friedrich Nietzsche

When coming up with a title for this song I stumbled upon the book *The Unbearable Lightness of Being* by Milan Kundera. After a quick skimming, I realized it had nothing to do with my lyrics, but I noticed the name Mefisto and was intrigued. After researching its origin and meaning, I knew I had to use it.

These lyrics captured a period of despair when I knew my problem, had the solution, but did nothing except wallow in self-pity and resentment.

What should I be pissed about today?

This attitude is the essence of a self-fulfilling prophecy.

A co-worker once said to me, "I can already tell it's going to be a bad day."

"Well, then don't act surprised and complain when it happens," I replied.

He was shocked at my response, an illustration of how blind we can be to our role in self-fulfilling prophecies.

By the media, by all the thoughts I'm thinking of
Overstimulated, can't concentrate, and I'm feeling numb

Imagine a dial in which the 12 o'clock position equals numb. As the knob turns clockwise, the amount of stimulation increases.

I often find myself at the moment right before the dial hits noon, feeling overwhelmed to the point of resignation.

When will it end?
Losing hope, reminiscing of Robin Williams again

If I'm after fame and fortune, and here is a person who had all of that and more, yet still checked out, what hope is there for me?

I am aware that having talent, money, and adoration by themselves won't guarantee happiness. However, there seems to be hope in that they *could*. It's an illusory, perhaps dangerous notion, but it can keep one moving forward.

Les Brown said that we all know a million dollars won't make us happy, but we all want to find out for ourselves.

I wonder if I'll ever "find out." But it's a disquieting notion given how unlikely fame and fortune are to produce happiness, and for that reason, I occasionally hope that I never do.

I'll cross that bridge if I get there. For now, I'll keep moving. Idle hands do the devil's work.

I'd trade a year for a moment to breathe

I used to think, "If things would just stop for a moment, I could catch my breath." What I realized over time was that for "things" to stop or slow down, I'd have to swim as fast or faster than the current of life.

Hello darkness, my old friend
I came to talk to, talk to you again

"Hello darkness, my old friend. I've come to talk with you again." – Simon & Garfunkel, "The Sound of Silence"

(I try) But my head is bursting
Chronically controlled by demonically possessive urges

If I believed in demons, it'd be a lot easier to explain why I willfully engage in the abysmal pleasures of self-destruction.

Perhaps this is the cost of free will, but I certainly don't feel like I'm "choosing" these pernicious desires.

It's for the better I don't shed the surface
You don't really want to know
What sits below this heavy burden

Fear of judgment, ridicule, and shame are a few reasons for not wanting to discuss this heavy burden. I also think it's to protect my ego.

If I discuss these thoughts and desires, I risk discovering that they aren't as irredeemable as I thought. This would not only make it harder to engage in cognitive distortions like catastrophizing but would alter my sense of purpose and identity.

I don't mean to be so candid when
I talk about my resignation letter to be handed in

I never thought I'd be so open about dealing with my depression and battling suicidal thoughts. Even writing these lines makes me cringe.

I've always felt that people who talk about being depressed are just crying for attention. On some level, I suppose that's the point. If you're drowning, quietly sinking is probably the least effective way of getting rescued.

While I never anticipated writing songs so personal, I'm glad I have. It's cathartic, and knowing others have benefited from hearing them makes it worth it.

WORK HARDER ON YOURSELF

Is that all the job pays or all the job pays you?
If you want more money, create more val-you
Don't get paid based on time despite popular opinion
But rather you get paid for the value that you put in it

If it's easy do it easy, if it's hard do it hard
Just get it done, just kick it in start
You can't change what's around you, and that's nothing new
But you can change yourself, and you can change what you do

Some have it bad; some have it great
But either way, you can't change the sun or the rain
So what's that to say? Well, it's to say this:
A better life awaits when you throw away your blame list

You're better off without it's
Not what happens that determines your future
But what you do about it

Don't wish for less problems
Wish for more skills
More skills to solve them

It makes all the difference when
You do something different and focus on your discipline
To have more, become more
And that's how you get a good foot in the front door

Is that all the job pays or all the job pays you?
If you want more money, create more val-you
Don't get paid based on time despite popular opinion
But rather you get paid for the value that you put in it

Learn to work harder on yourself than you do on your job
And in due time, you'll be moving along
Don't try to change the soil, never mind the seed
A propensity to change until you get it right is all you need

See your target, aim
We get paid for bringing value to the marketplace
So, if you want to double your income
Then double your value, double your wisdom

Oh, you're going to go on strike for more money?
Well, you can't get rich by demand buddy
You're going to wait for a raise?
Man, it's easier to climb the ladder rather than wait

So develop your philosophy, skills, the graces
Work on your attitude, health, your language
If you double your value, could you earn more?
The answer is, "OF COURSE!"

Is that all the job pays or all the job pays you?
If you want more money, create more val-you
Don't get paid based on time despite popular opinion
But rather you get paid for the value that you put in it

WORK HARDER ON YOURSELF

"Whatever you reap is what you've sown."
– Earl Shoaff

Jim Rohn is widely considered to be the founding father of motivational speaking.

His quotes have hit me so hard that my brain grew a penis and jerked itself off. I say this tongue-in-cheek but also seriously.

If a picture is worth a thousand words, his quotes are worth a thousand dollars.

I can tell you in two words how a lowly goober like myself got to interview magician David Copperfield inside his mansion and play with his toys: Jim Rohn.

Most of the lines in this song are direct quotes or adaptations from two of Rohn's seminars: *How to Have Your Best Year Ever* and *The Day That Turns Your Life Around.*

Is that all the job pays or all the job pays you?

At age twenty-five, Rohn had a life-changing conversation with his mentor Earl Shoaff. The first line of the chorus was inspired by their talk:

"You've been working six years, Mr. Rohn. How come you're not doing better?" Shoaff asked.

"This is all the company pays," Rohn answered.

"Well, that's not true."

"No, this is my paycheck. This is all the company pays."

"No, this is all the company pays you. Doesn't the company pay two, three, four, five times this amount to other people?"

"Well, yes,"

"Well, then this isn't all the company pays. This is all they pay you. If you qualified, wouldn't your income grow two, three, four, five times?"

"I suppose."

"Then we don't have to work on the company. We have to work on you."

If you want more money, create more val-you

Value + You = Val-you

If it's easy do it easy, if it's hard do it hard

"If it's easy do it easy. If it's hard do it hard. Just get it done." – Earl Shoaff.

Shoaff's quote, by forcing me to accept the task at hand as it is, not as I wish it to be, has saved me so much energy and needless suffering.

There are proper times and places for venting, but bitching and getting stressed over a shitty job or unfavorable situation only adds to your negative experience.

You can't change what's around you, and that's nothing new
But you can change yourself, and you can change what you do

"You can't change the seasons, but you can change yourself. That's how life gets better for you. Not by chance, but by change." – Jim Rohn.

So what's that to say? Well, it's to say this:
A better life awaits when you throw away your blame list

Rohn says how he used to have a long list of reasons for why he wasn't doing well called, "Reasons for Not Looking

Good."

He blamed the government, taxes, prices, weather, traffic, and about eight other things.

When Mr. Shoaff asked why he wasn't doing so well, Jim gleefully went over his list. Shoaff was patient, waited until he finished, then bluntly replied, "There's just one problem with your list Mr. Rohn. You ain't on it!"

Wayne Dyer in his abridged audiobook for *Pulling Your Own Strings* explains that in his counseling sessions he had clients write down everyone and everything responsible for why they weren't where they felt they should be. Family, education, lack of money, and the government were typical answers.

He'd then ask a very critical question, "Now what?"

As Rohn said, "For things to change, *you've* got to change."

It's not what happens that determines your future
But what you do about it

"It's not what happens to you, but how you react to it that matters." – Epictetus

Don't wish for less problems, wish for more skills

"Don't wish it was easier, wish you were better. Don't wish for less problems, wish for more skills. Don't wish for less challenge, wish for more wisdom." – Jim Rohn

To have more, become more

"You can have more than you've got, because you can become more than you are." – Jim Rohn

Learn to work harder on yourself than you do on your job

"Learn to work harder on yourself than you do on your job. If you work hard on your job, you can make a living, but if you work hard on yourself, you'll make a fortune." – Jim Rohn

Don't try to change the soil, never mind the seed
A propensity to change until you get it right is all you need

"Don't try to change the sea. Don't change the soil. Don't change the sunshine. Don't change the rain. Let the miracle of what's available work for you, and start working on the inside." – Jim Rohn

We get paid for bringing value to the marketplace

Value makes the difference in results.
     To summarize one of Rohn's talks, "We don't get paid for time. We get paid for the value we bring to the marketplace. Is it possible to become twice as valuable to the marketplace and make twice as much money in the same time? The answer: of course."
     "The reality is: if you're not very valuable to the marketplace you don't get much money."

Oh, you're going to go on strike for more money?
Well, you can't get rich by demand buddy
You're going to wait for a raise?
Man, it's easier to climb the ladder rather than wait

Rohn talks about America being an economic ladder to climb, and how you move up it as you increase your value. He then plays out two objections:

"I'll go on strike for more money," the guy said.

"Well, you can't get rich by demand," Rohn replied.

"Then I'll wait for a raise."

"I'm telling you it's easier to climb rather than to wait."

"Well, I was a hard worker. But I was working on my job, not on myself. I'm telling you if you'll learn that simple little principle and start the process today, latest tomorrow – I'll give you tonight to think it over. If you'll start working harder on yourself than you do on your job."

This is a direct sample of Rohn's voice from his seminar, *How to Have Your Best Year Ever*.

I used to focus a lot on saving money. I was spending just 5 dollars a day on food, not per meal, per day. That's when I realized I had to shift my focus from saving to *creating*, from prevention to an expansion mindset.

I had to figure out ways to become more valuable to the marketplace. What product or service could I offer? What skills did I have? What could I acquire that I could market?

We're always building momentum towards a good or bad habit.

It's shameful to admit, but I've had jobs where I just derped through the day. "They don't respect me. This is beneath me. This isn't what I want to do anyway."

Those were justifications I used for my poor work ethic. These kinds of excuses may be truisms, but the problem is that those negative attitudes carried over into life outside of work.

Instead of focusing on my goals in the evening, I'd be too tired or unmotivated from such a "stressful" day to do anything positive.

As the Zen saying goes, "How you do anything is how you do everything."

That's why it is essential to lay it on at work, so when you get home, you'll lay it on with your passions. Not only will you get further with your vision but you'll also be more valuable to your employer.

I'll leave you with one last brain-stroking story from Jim Rohn.

After Shoaff set him straight about how much the company paid, Rohn complained how things "cost too much."

Shoaff gracefully replied, "No, you can't afford them. You know we put some of the valuable things on the high shelf so you can't get them until you qualify. If you want the things on the higher shelf, *you've got to stand on the books you read.*"

FEELING FRIDAY ON TUESDAY

A friend posted a meme that said, "Nothing fucks up your Friday like realizing it's only Tuesday."

I was baffled when I read this because, for starters, Friday isn't real. It's a human construct. You won't find it laying under a rock in nature.

Second, whatever emotional states you experience on Friday can be accessed ANY day.

So why do so many of us fall prey to this Weekend Warrior narrative? I believe it comes down to this:

1. *It's not socially acceptable.* Try going into work on Tuesday with a smile and doing a little dance. People will be confused and interrogate you. "What are you so happy about? Did somebody get laid?"

2. *Fear.* We want to avoid criticism and ridicule, so we don't permit ourselves to feel happy in the present. Unless, of course, it's presently Friday.

We are raised from birth to believe that happiness comes from external sources such as movies, marriage, a degree, sports, drugs, material possessions, achievements, and so on.

Society would have you believe that you can't be happy by virtue of declaration or of your own will. We are continually looking for an outside solution to an inside problem.

I shared this with a friend, and she replied, "Yeah, but on Friday I know that I get to sleep in, go out if I want, and see my family."

These are objective facts (reality), but her feelings about these facts are judgments (perception).

Feelings don't change reality.

However, feelings can change how we perceive our lives. This is the key to *Feeling Friday on Tuesday*.

Our emotional state is basically the product of this formula:

Observation + Beliefs About Observation = Internal State (Feelings)

For example, my friend observes it's a Tuesday. She believes Tuesdays suck. Therefore, she feels unhappy.

Alternatively, when she observes it's a Friday, she feels happy because she believes Fridays are sweet.

But what's changed? She works on *both* days.

The difference is in her beliefs about what she observes. That's why it's so crucial to pay attention to how you're mentally filling in the formula.

Shakespeare wrote, "There is nothing either good or bad, but thinking makes it so." You don't have to spend four days feeling miserable just to enjoy one.

Happiness starts with giving yourself permission to be happy. You can only attain it in the present. You will never be as happy as you are right now. Yes, *right now*. A friend challenged me on this. Our conversation went as follows:

"What time is it?" I asked.

"It's 3:20 pm," he answered.

"OK, now what time is it?"

"It's 3:20 pm."

I paused for a moment…

"OK, what time is it right now?"

"Now it's 3:21 pm."

See my point? I'm not playing a silly semantics game.

You can think about the future and the past, but you can only *live* in the present moment. You don't need an external justification like "Friday" to experience positive emotions. Whatever you think you'll feel with the external justification you can feel without it. You only need to give yourself permission to do it.

Don't put off your happiness for a moment that may never arrive.

My Challenge to You

Regardless of what you do for a career or hobby, I encourage you to do something once a week that's outside of your comfort zone and release it publicly.

Perhaps it's a photo with a poem published every Wednesday.

Maybe it's reading a book and putting up a review every Sunday.

The goal isn't to have the flashiest photograph and passionate poem or detailed review with academic language.

The point is to cultivate an unwavering commitment that forces you to learn new things, build your skills, and leave you with a sense of accomplishment.

When you hold yourself accountable and develop a strong work ethic you can expect these benefits:

- More easily distinguish between the things you can and cannot control
- More resourceful with time, effort, and energy
- Deeper knowledge of self

Increased confidence in:

- Operating under stressful conditions
- Dealing with negative emotions
- Making the most of situations
- Overcoming self-limitations
- Taking initiative
- Meeting deadlines
- Taking on new challenges

Don't worry if you think you're not a "creative" type. Commit first and figure it out as you go. If you are the creative type but claim that you can't "force" your creativity, please know that is nothing more than a justification for failure and laziness.

As the saying goes, "Sometimes it's inspiration. Other times it's perspiration." Lo-fi is better than No-fi.

For those of you daring enough to take on the challenge, I'd love to hear about your journey. Please email me at hiphoptimism@gmail.com and tell me about your experience.

Your future is full of your present actions.

RECOMMENDING READING

Philosophy & Personal Development

• *The Day That Turns Your Life Around* by Jim Rohn

• *The 7 Habits of Highly Effective People: Powerful Lessons in Personal Change* by Stephen R. Covey

• *The Obstacle Is the Way: The Timeless Art of Turning Trials into Triumph* by Ryan Holiday

• *On the Shortness of Life: Life Is Long if You Know How to Use It (Penguin Great Ideas)* by Seneca and C. D. N. Costa

Relationships

• *Crucial Conversations: Tools for Talking When Stakes Are High* by Kerry Patterson, Joseph Grenny, Ron McMillan, and Al Switzler

• *Pulling Your Own Strings: Dynamic Techniques for Dealing with Other People and Living Your Life As You Choose* by Wayne W Dyer

• *The Way of the Superior Man: A Spiritual Guide to Mastering the Challenges of Women, Work, and Sexual Desire* by David Deida

Business & Finance

• *Sell or Be Sold: How to Get Your Way in Business and in Life* by Grant Cardone

• *The Richest Man in Babylon* by George S. Clason

www.ingramcontent.com/pod-product-compliance
Lightning Source LLC
Chambersburg PA
CBHW072015230526
45468CB00021B/1569